Mandala Animal Adult Coloring Book

Copyright 2019 Coloring World Books
All Rights Reserved

Find my other books here:
amazon.com/author/coloring-world-books

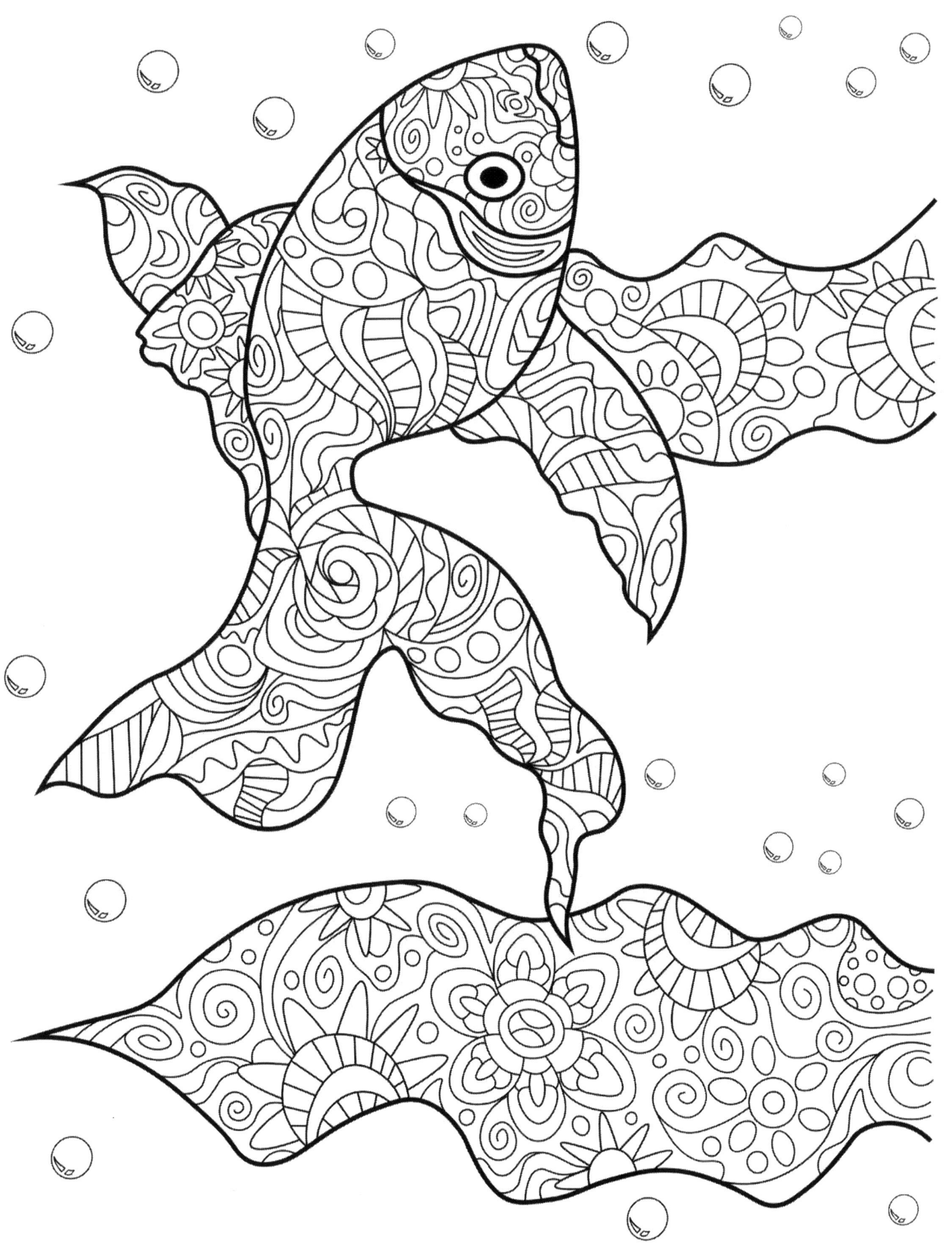

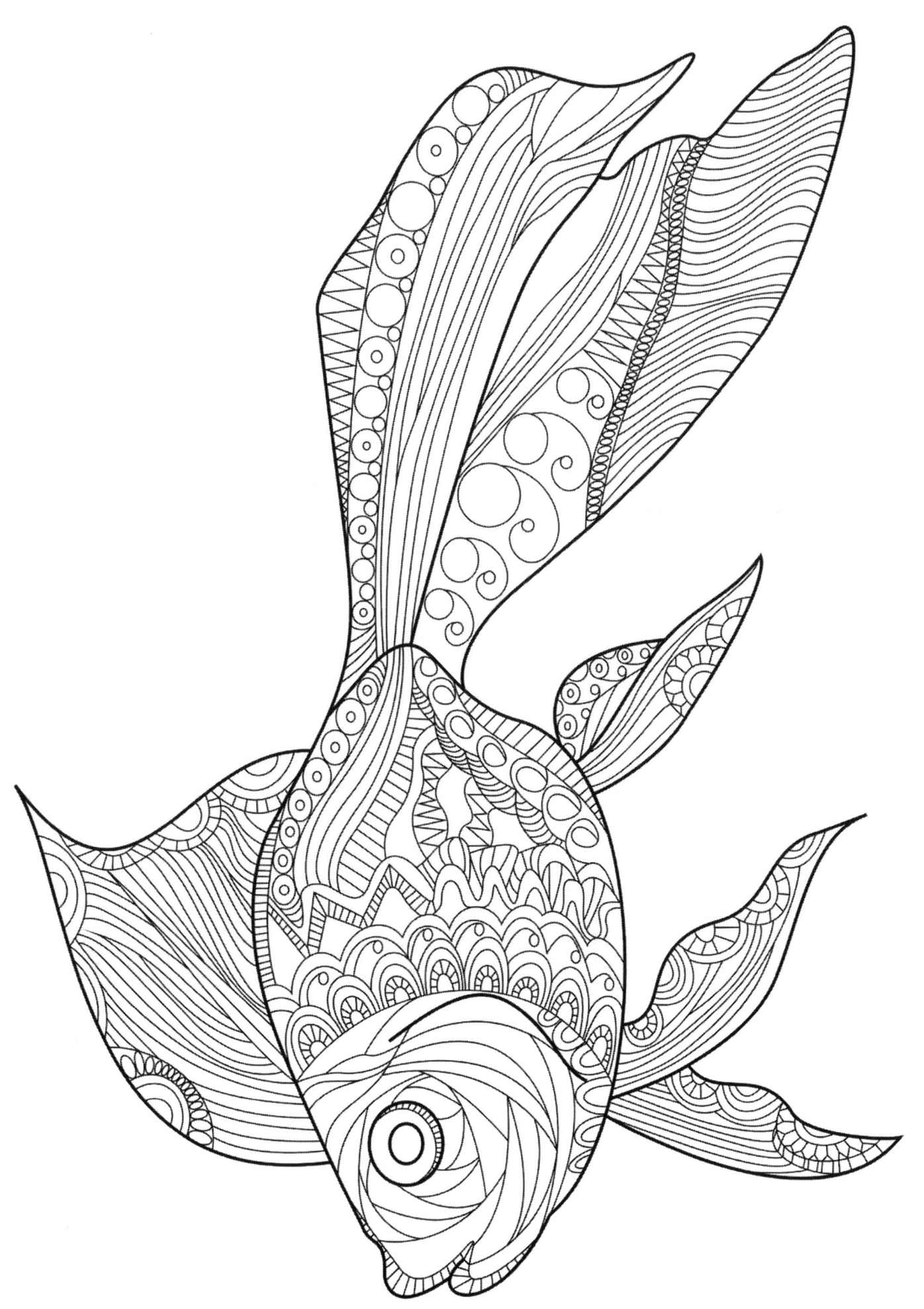

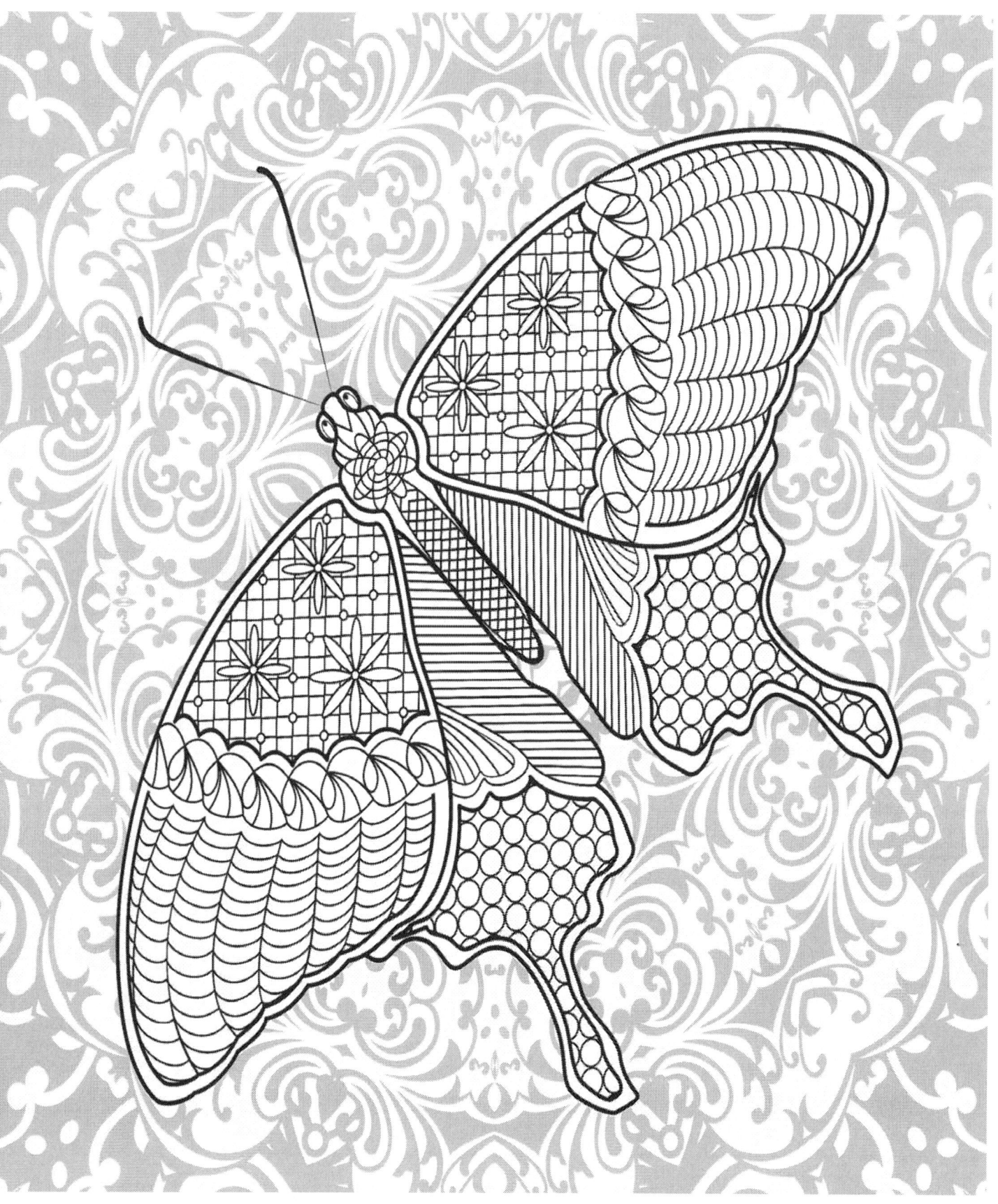

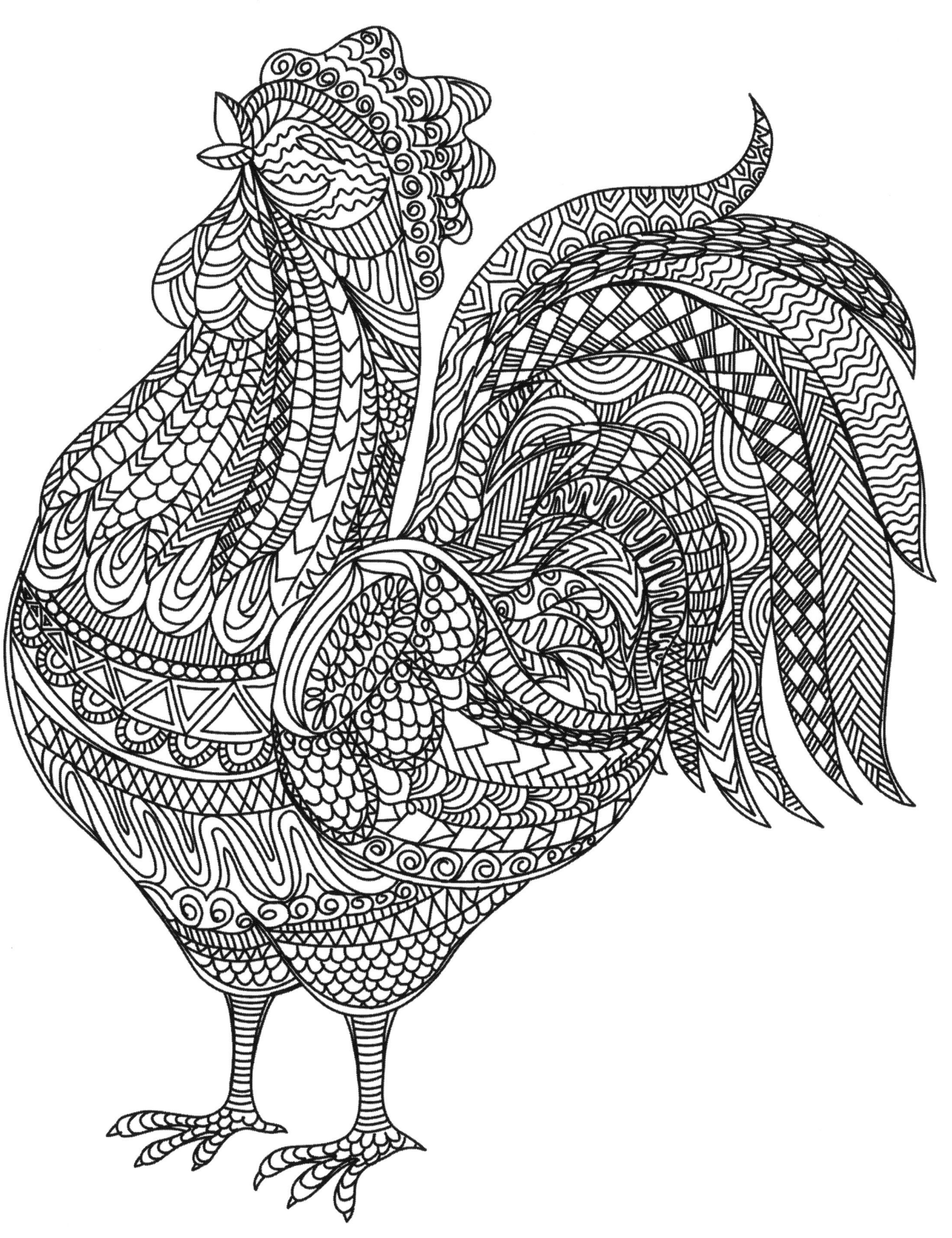

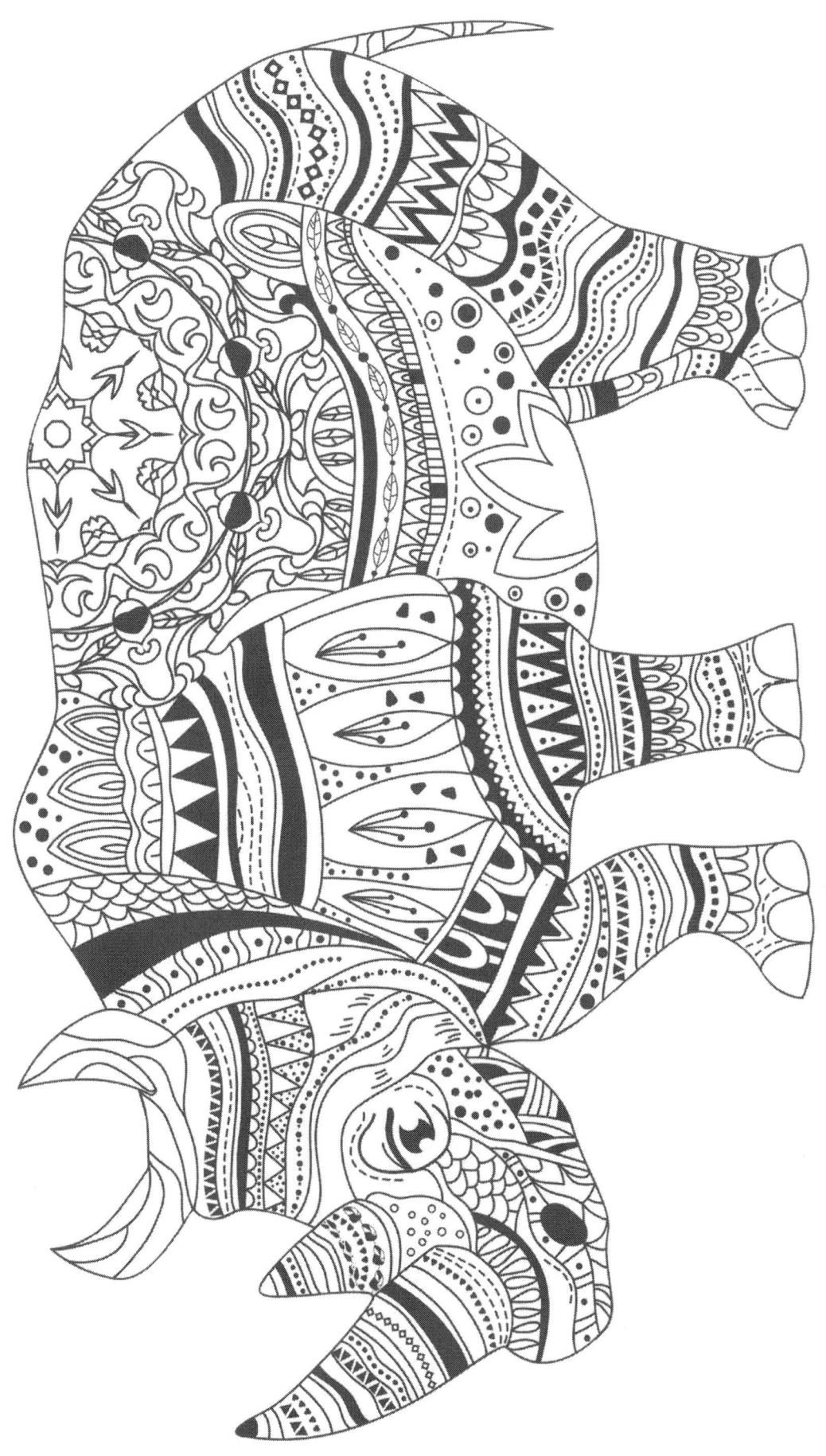

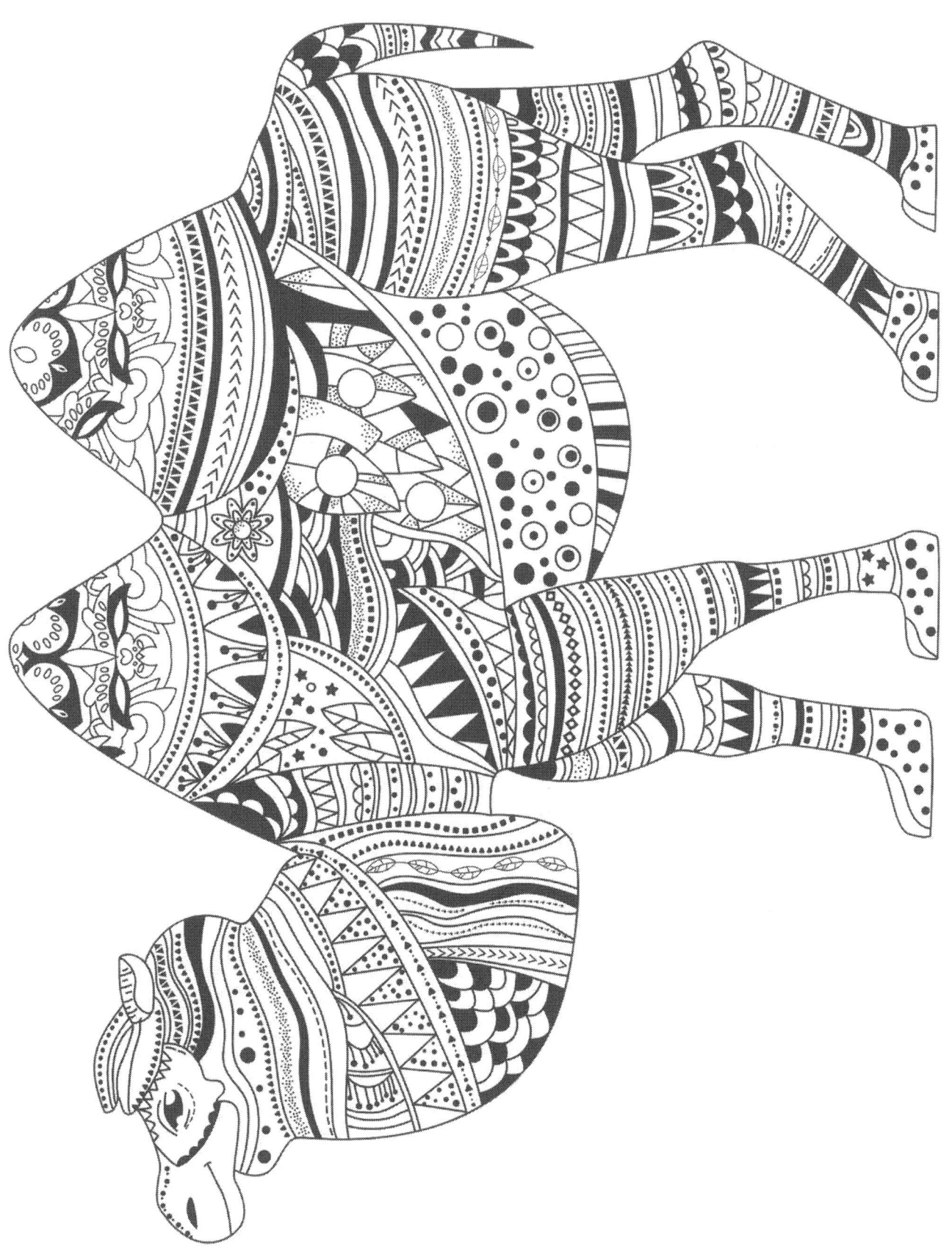

Color Test Page

Color Test Page

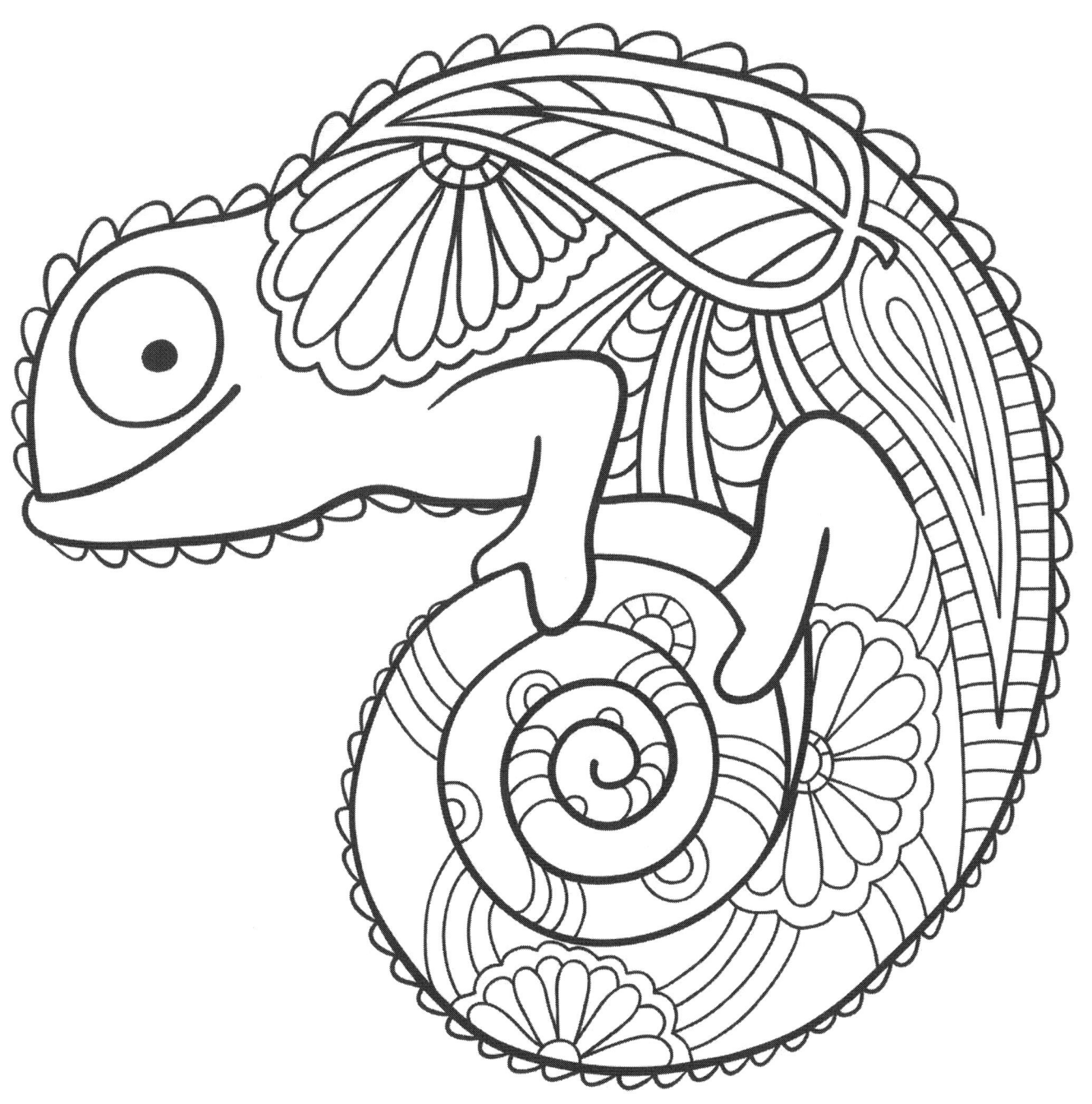

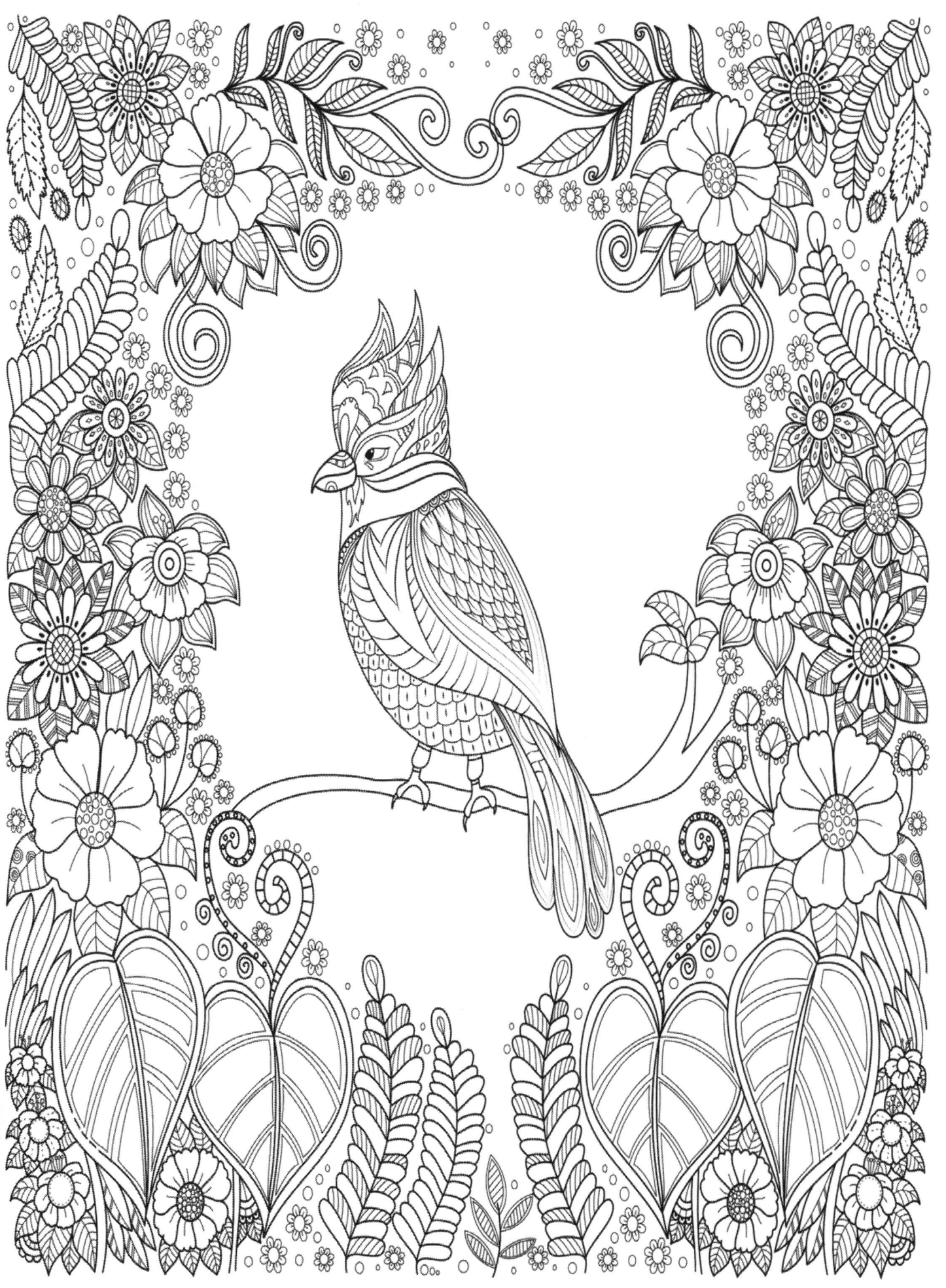

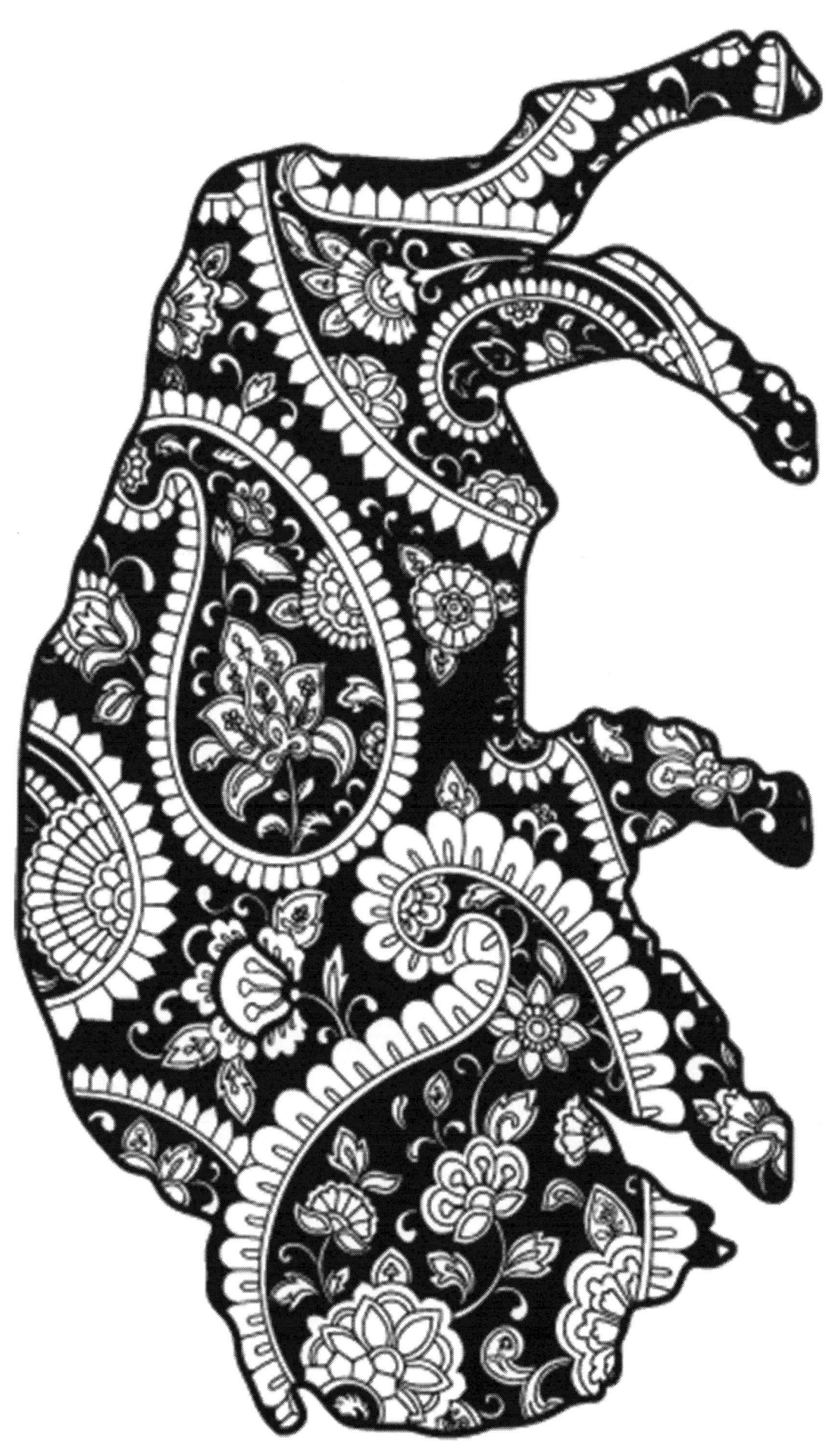

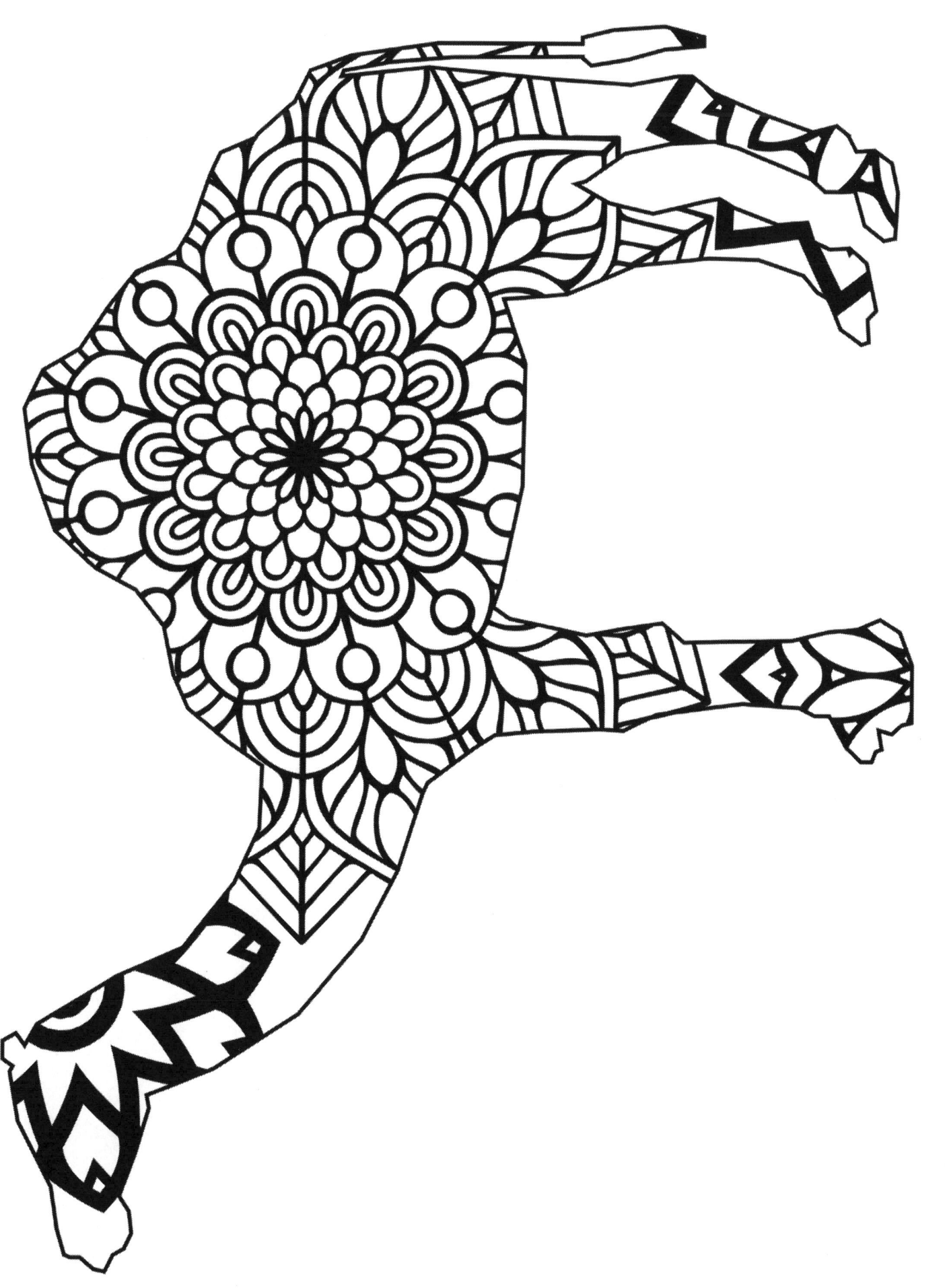

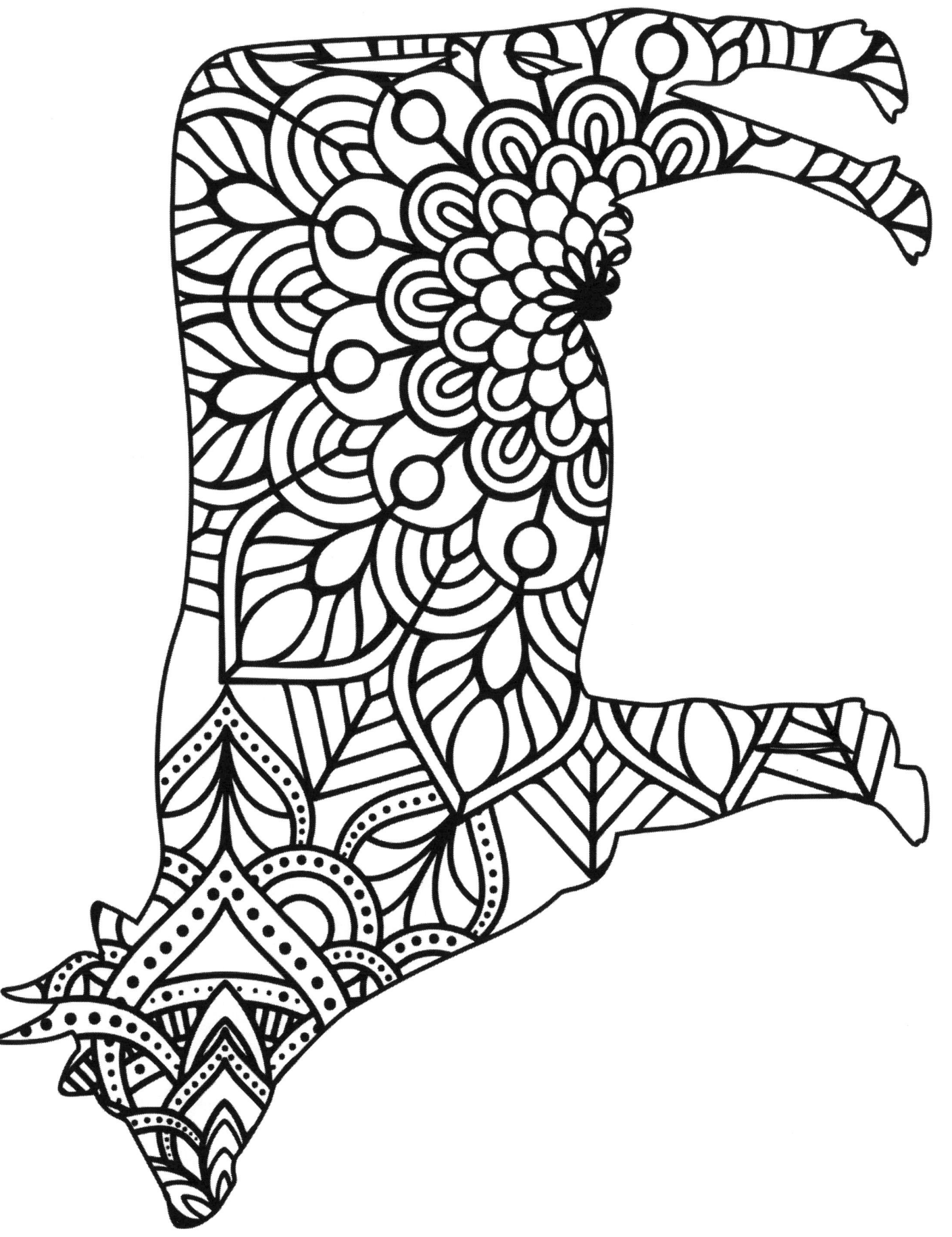

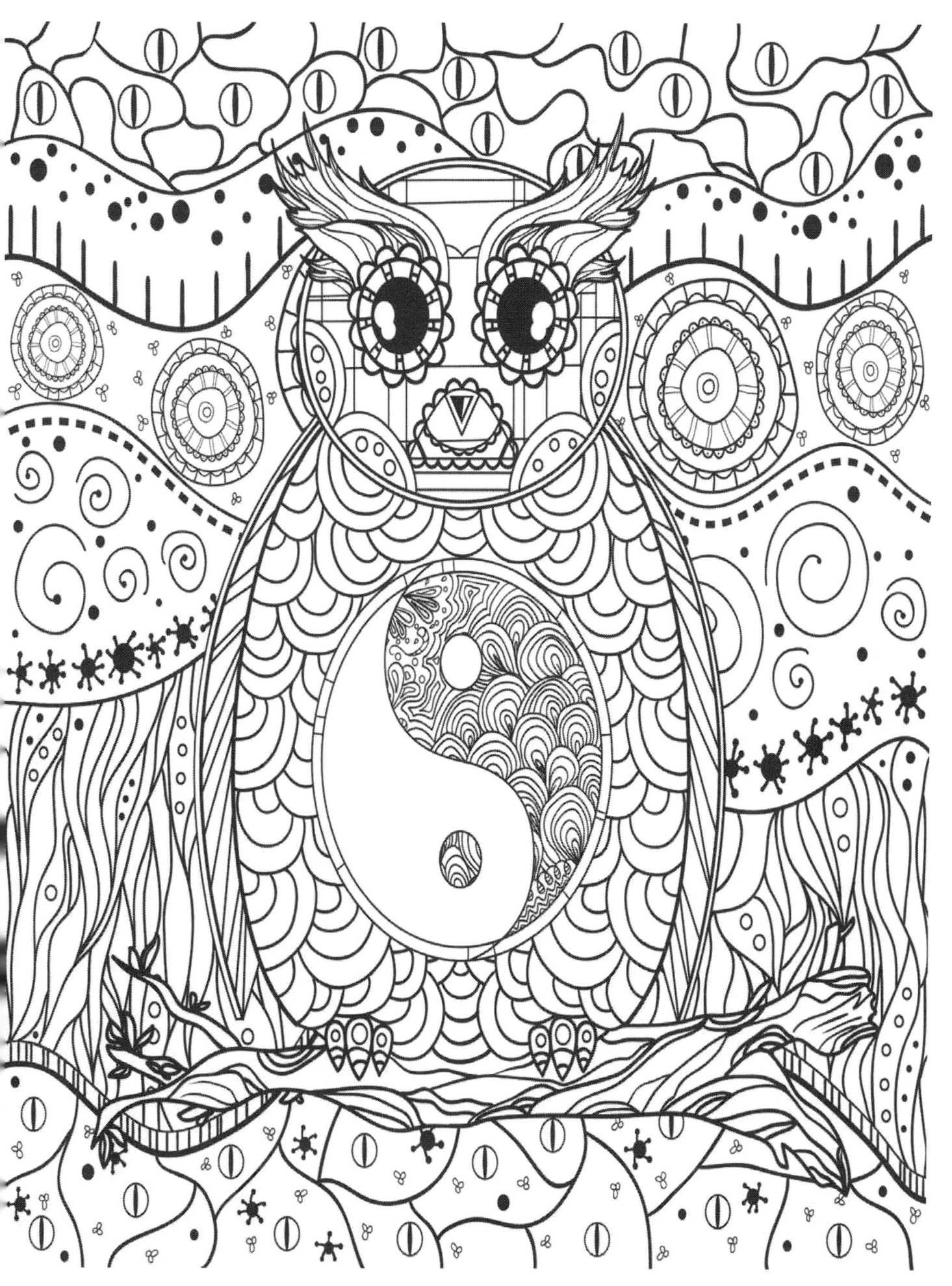

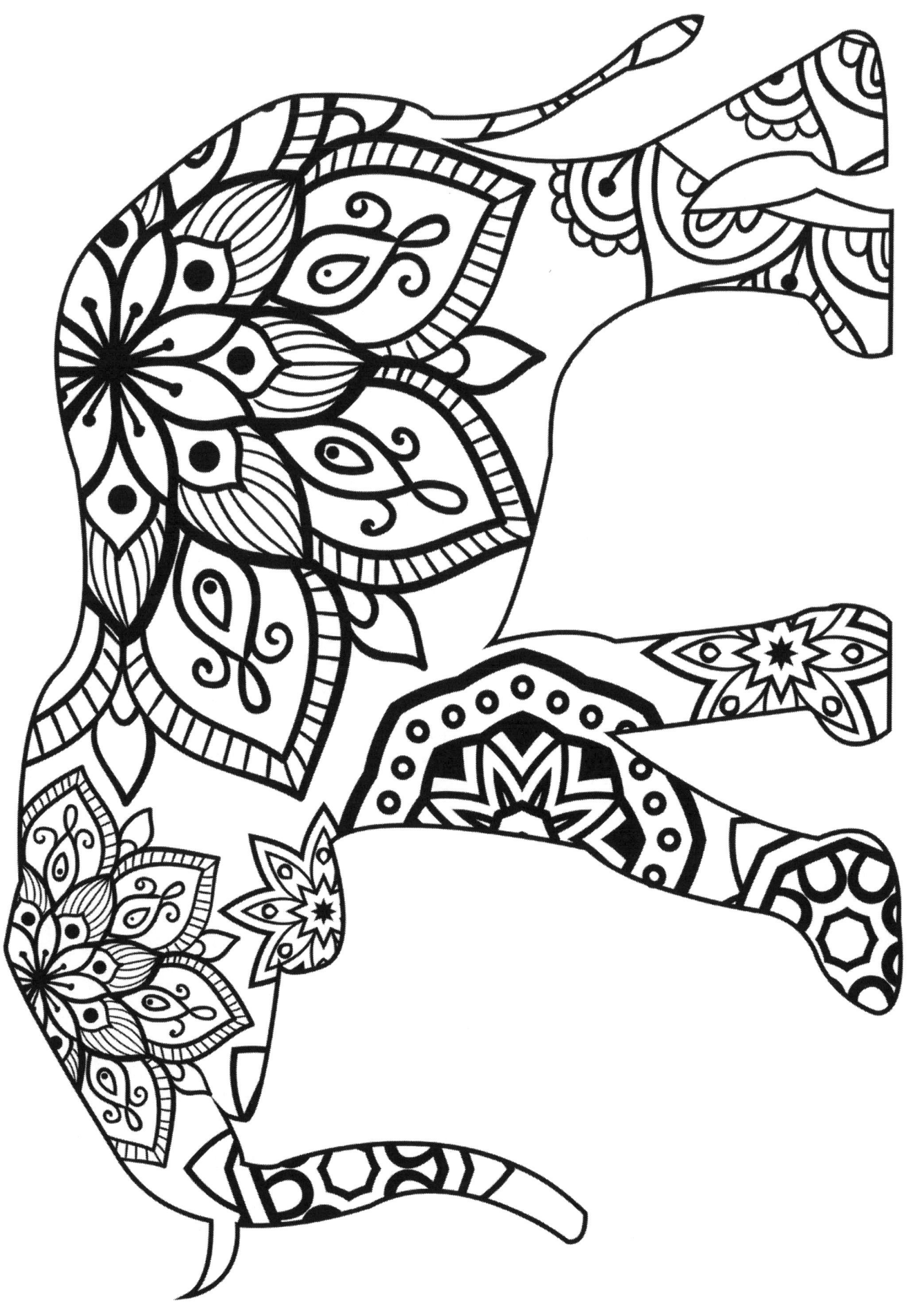

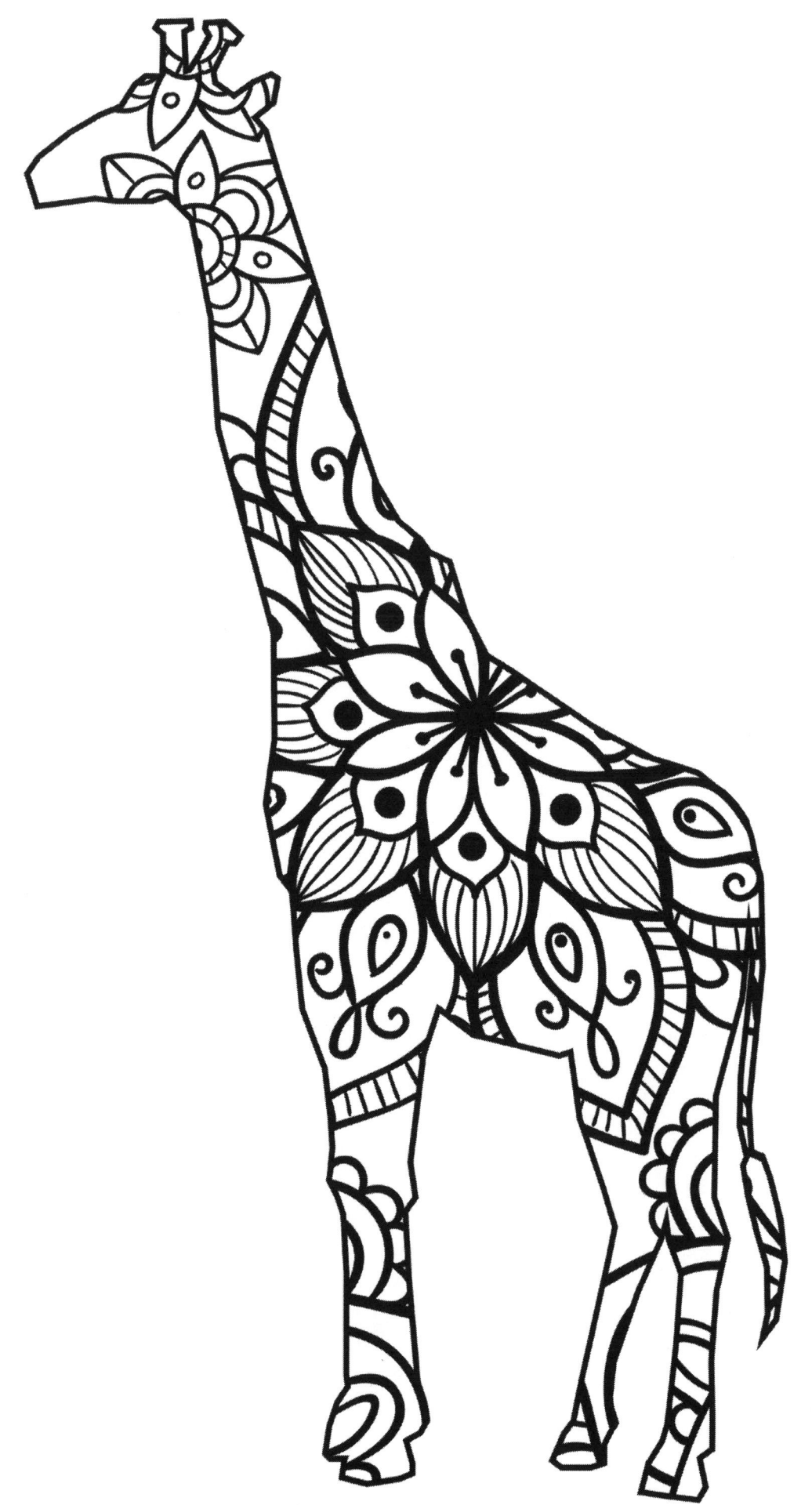

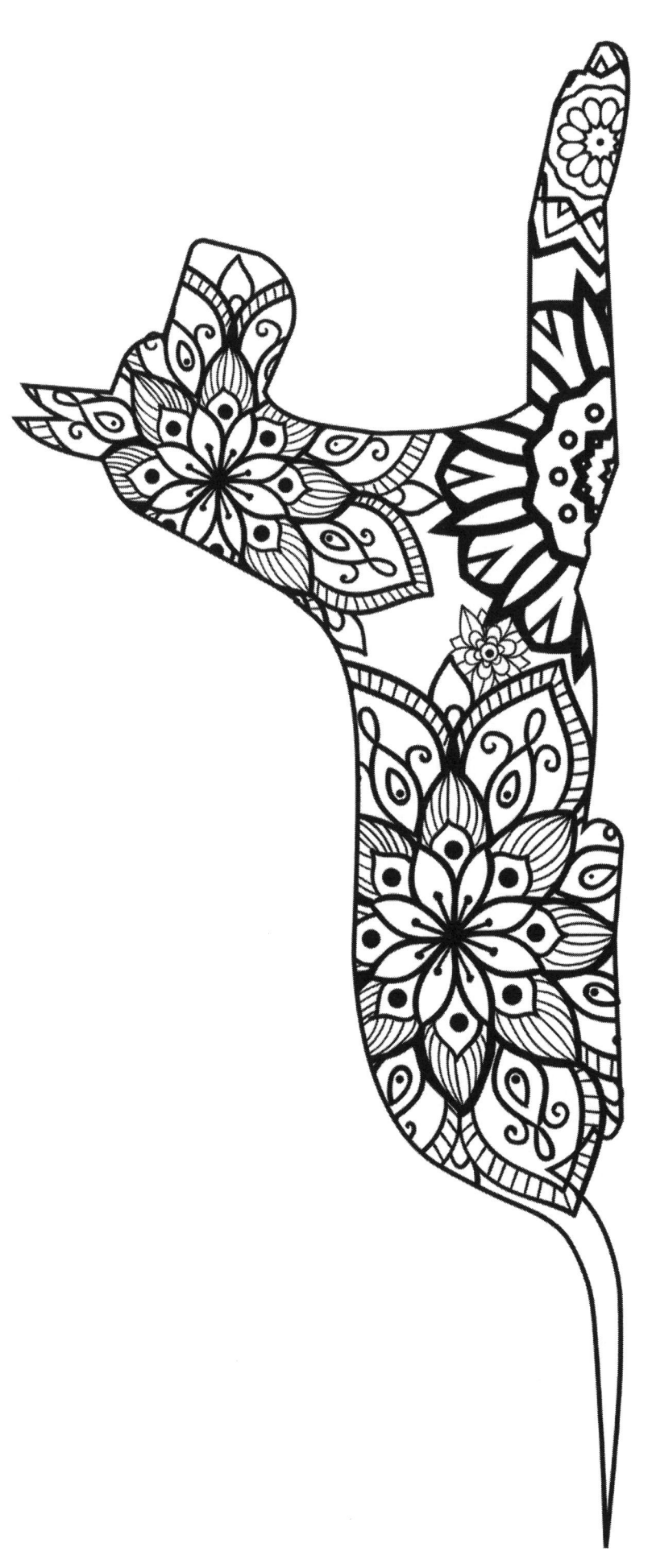

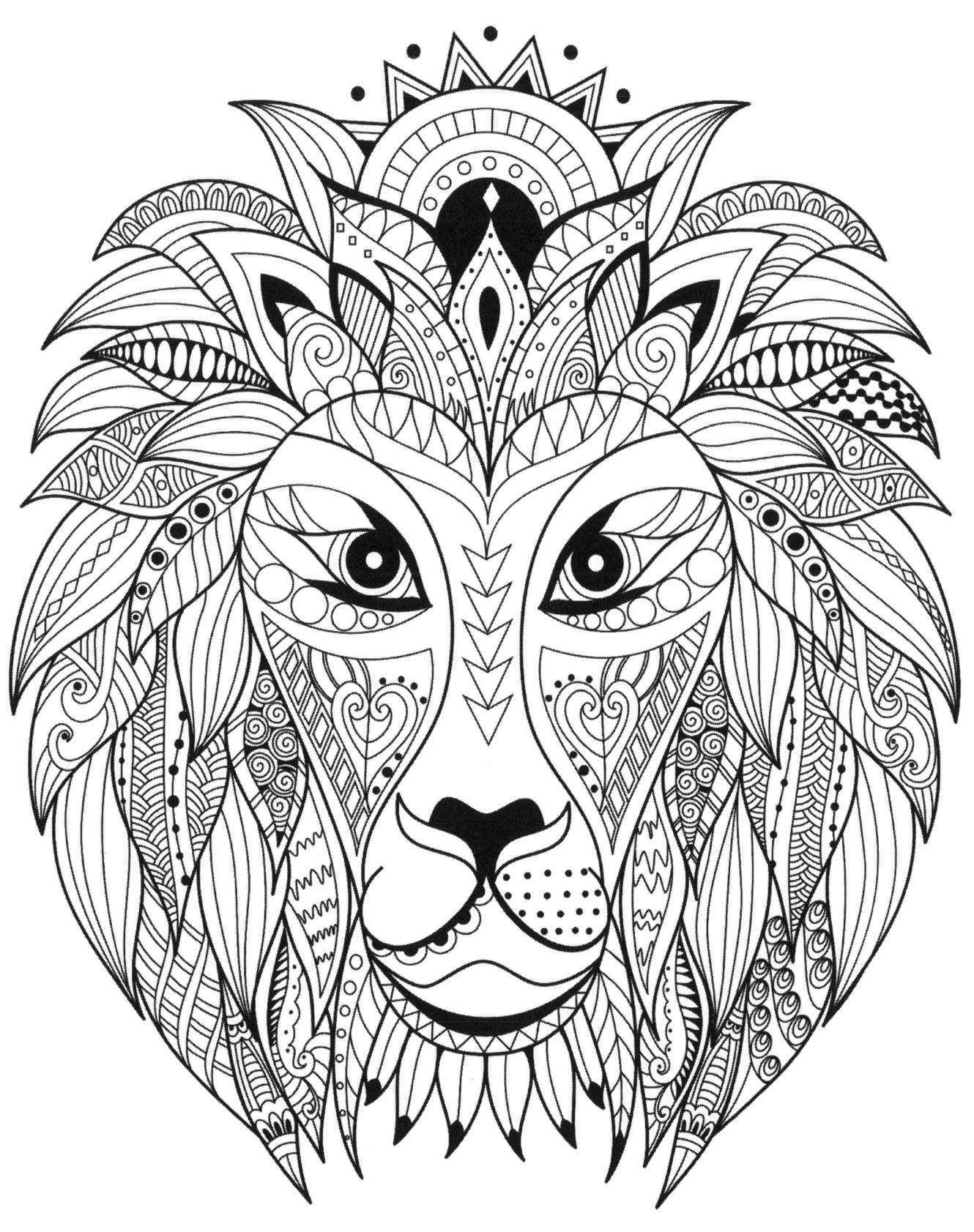

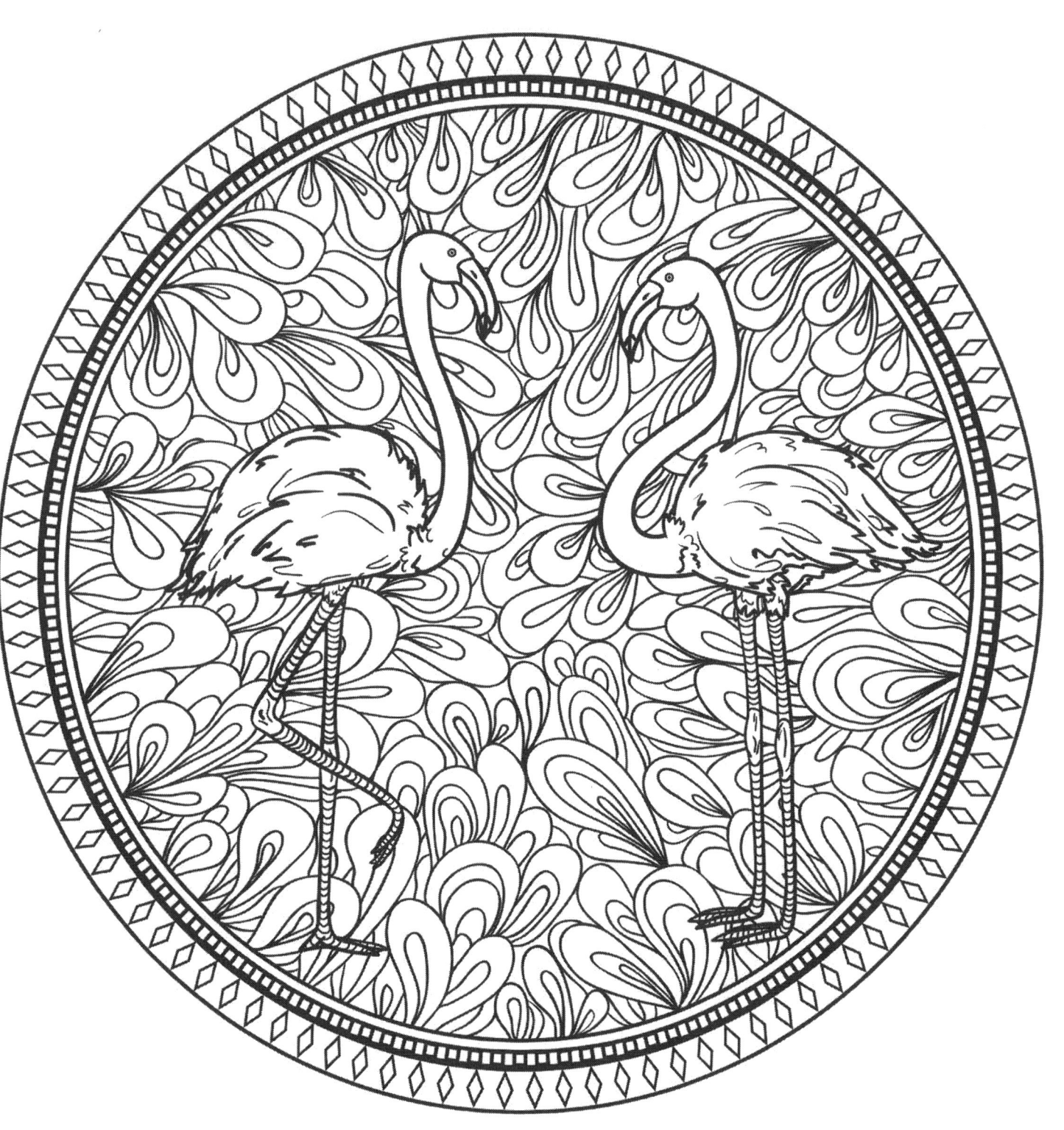

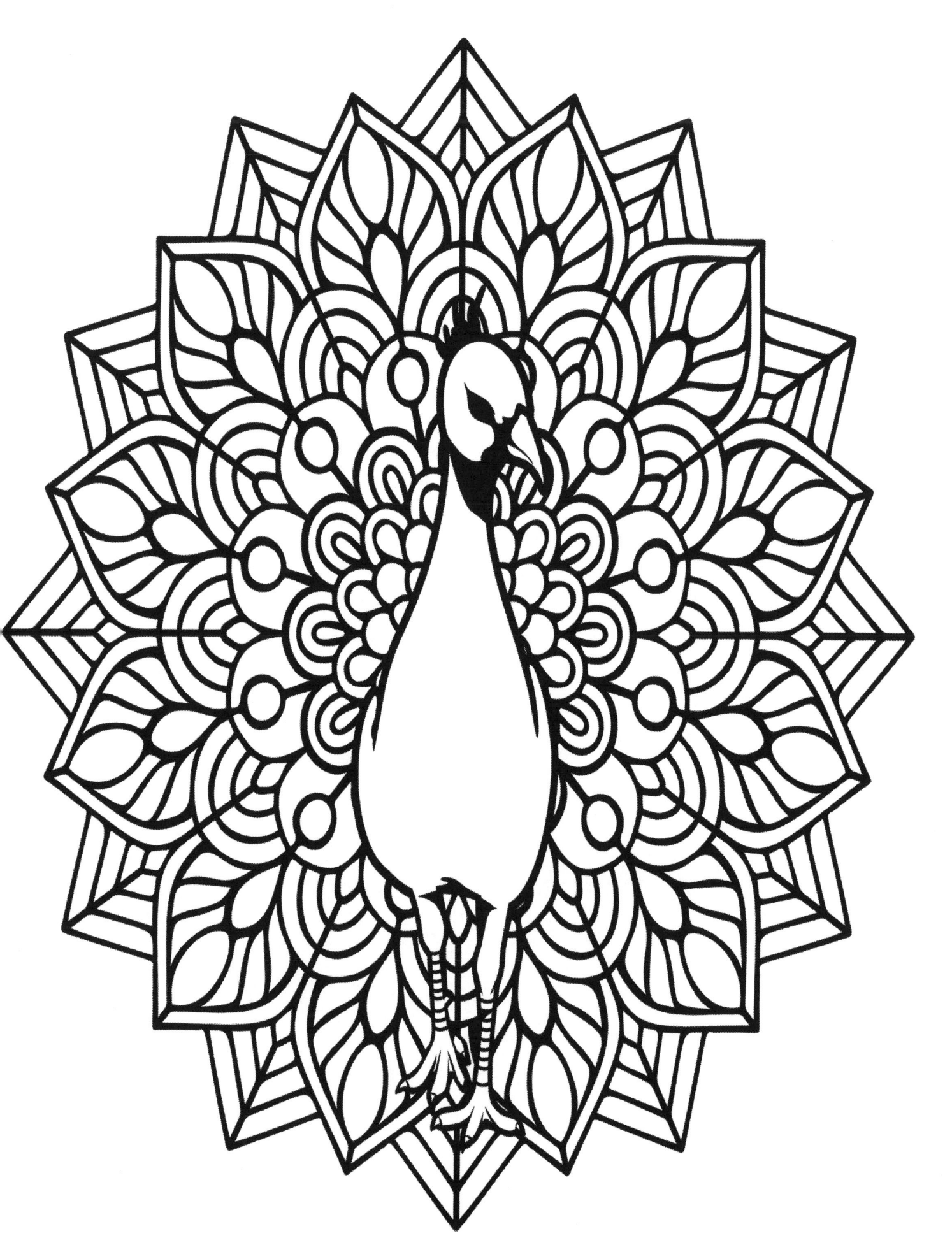

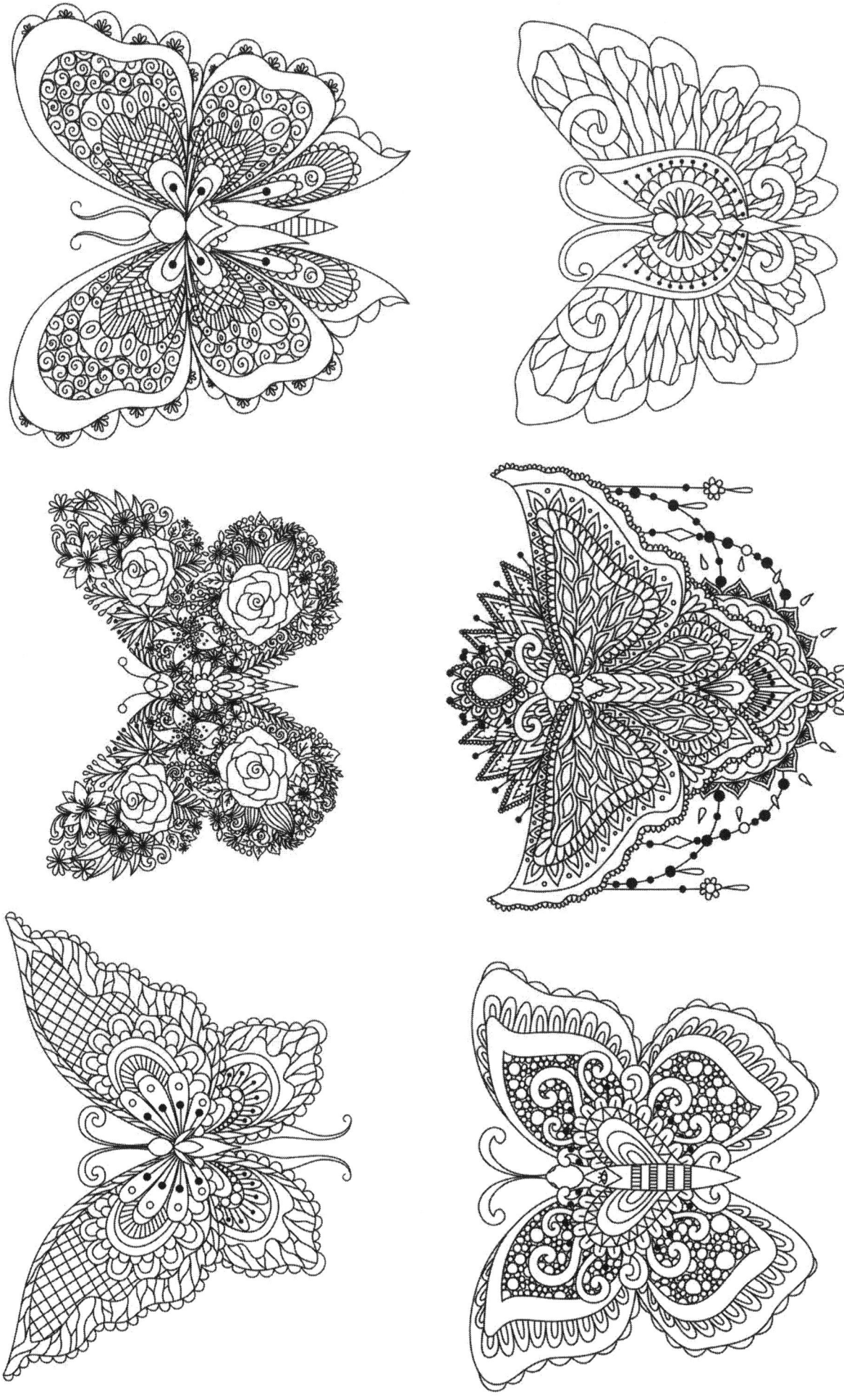

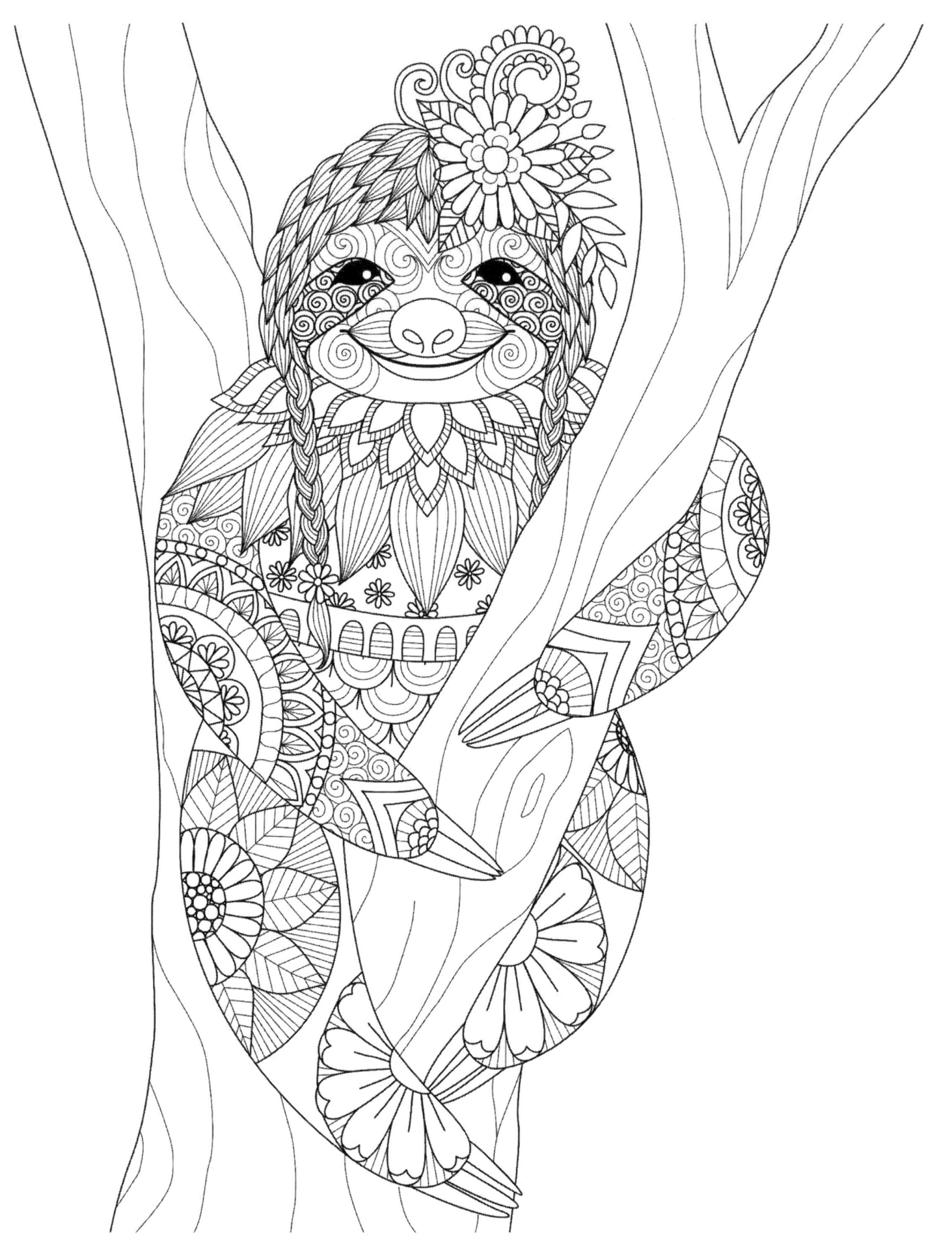

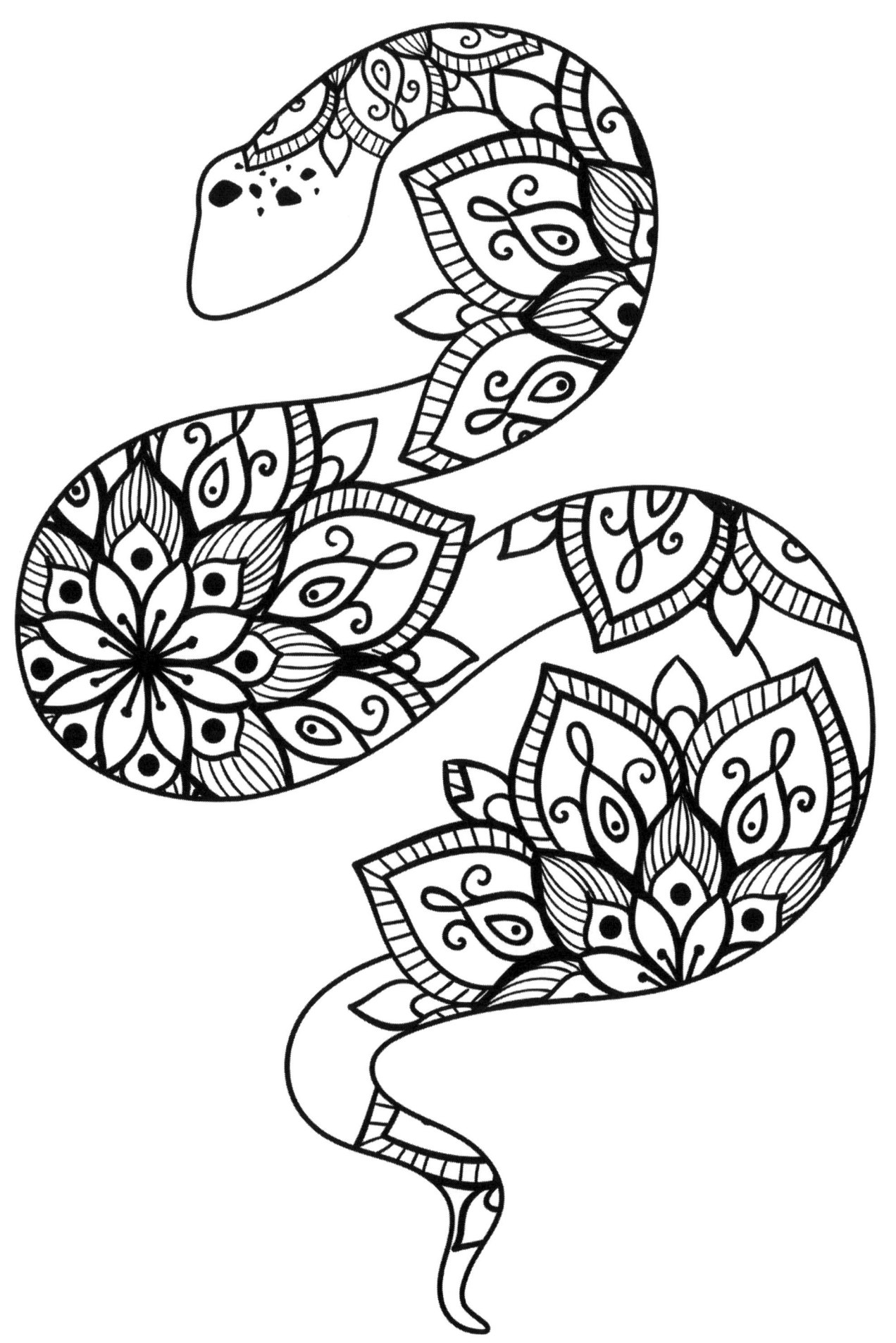

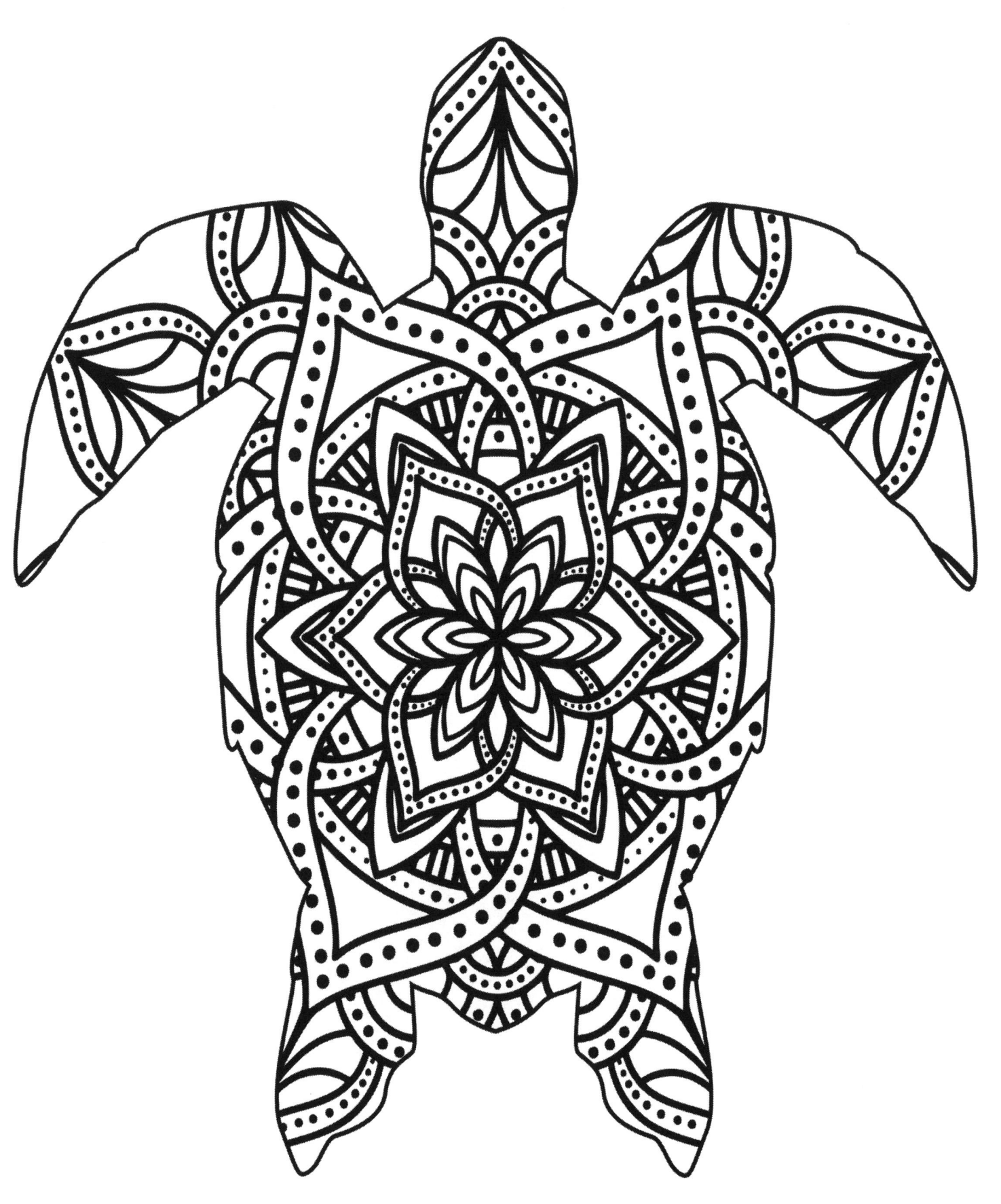

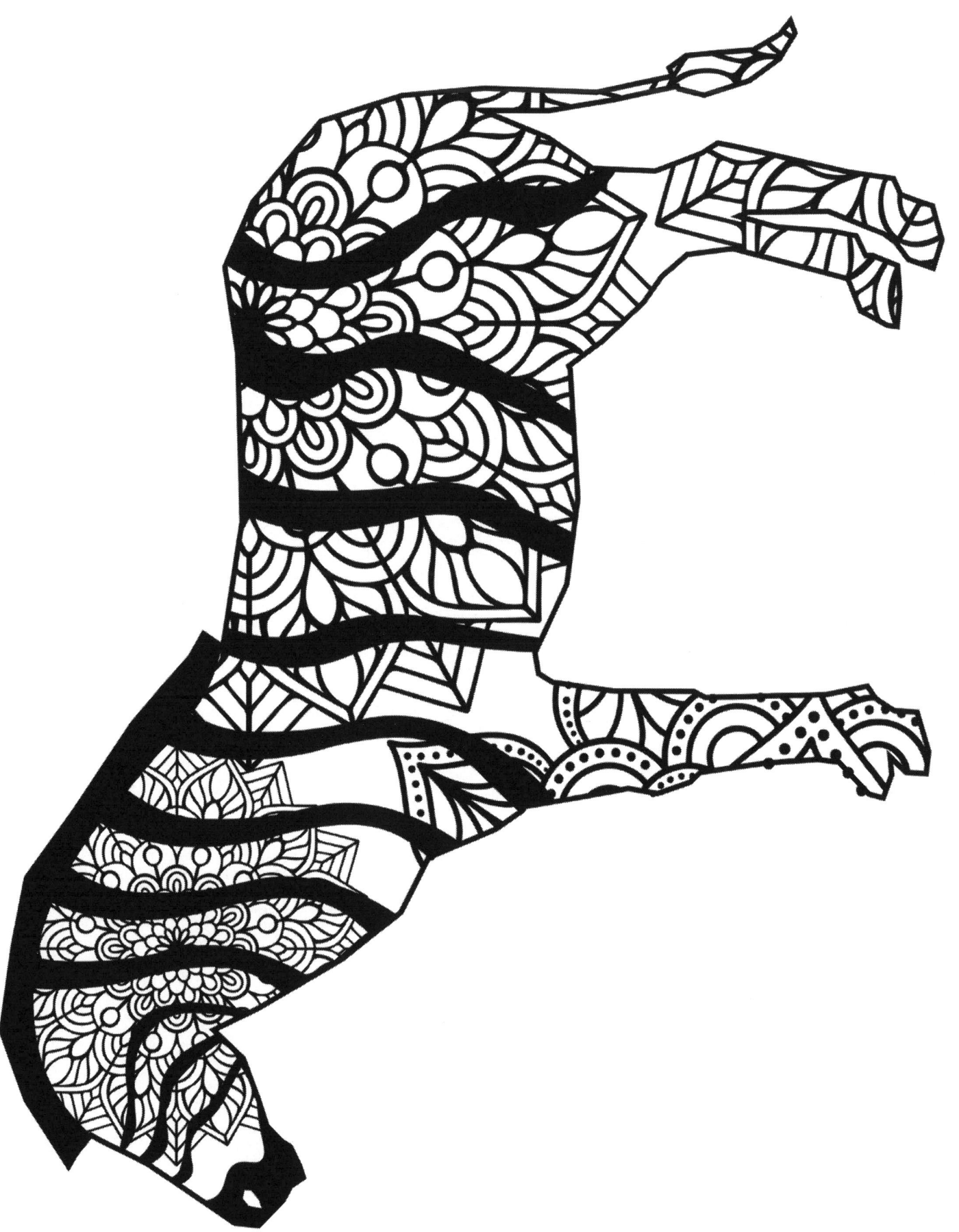

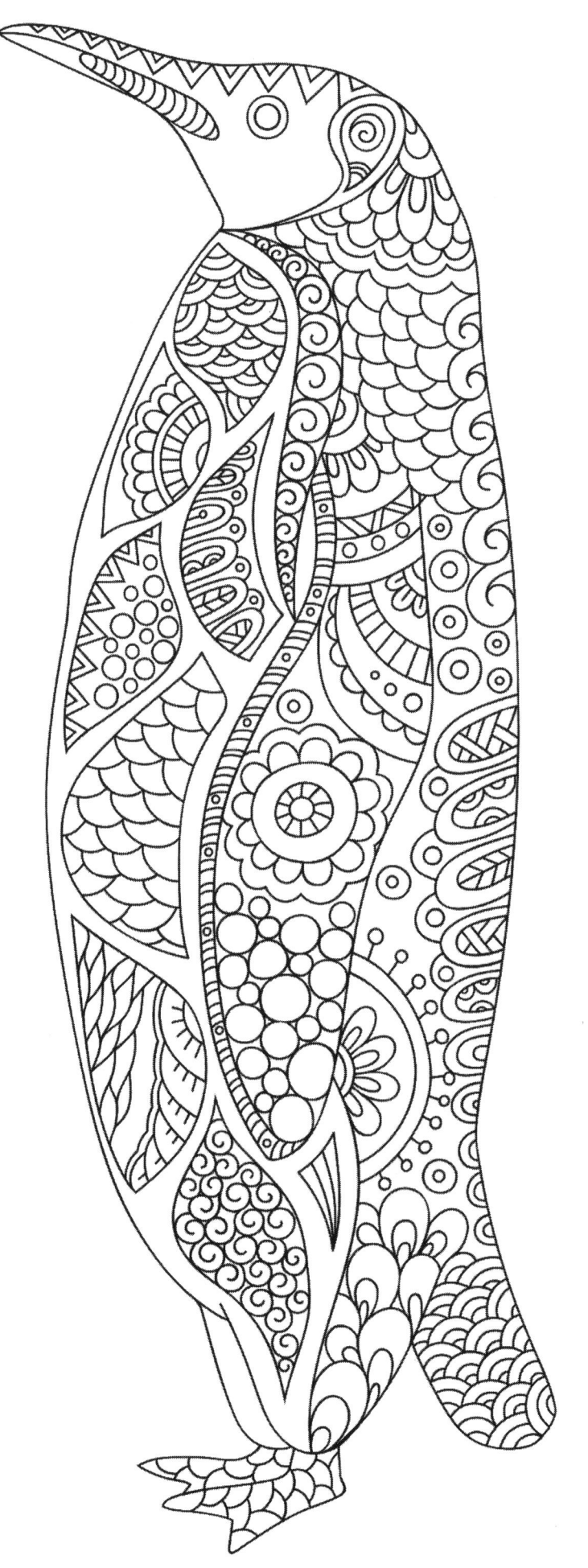

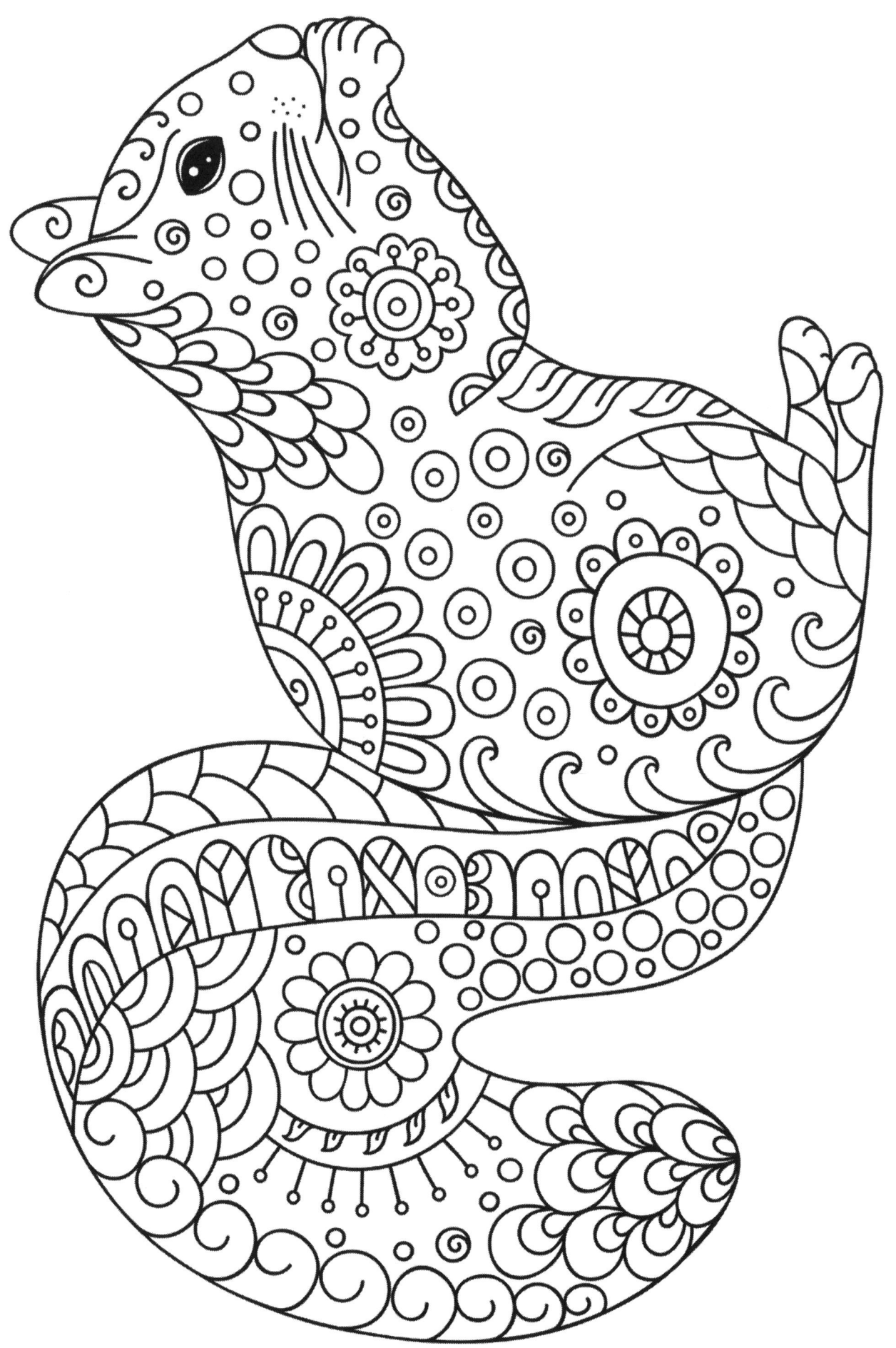

Made in the USA
Columbia, SC
28 March 2020